ICAEW

Financial Accounting and Reporting – IFRS

C000072033

TP06-17421-011

Ninth edition 2020

ISBN 9781 5097 3419 1

British Library Cataloguing-in-Publication Data

A catalogue record for this publication is available from the British Library

Published by

BPP Learning Media Ltd,
BPP House, Aldine Place,
142-144 Uxbridge Road,
London W12 8AA

www.bpp.com/learningmedia

Printed in the United Kingdom

Your learning materials, published by BPP Learning Media Ltd, are printed on paper obtained from traceable sustainable sources.

Welcome to BPP Learning Media's **Passcards** for ICAEW **Financial Accounting and Reporting – IFRS**.

- They **save you time**. Important topics are summarised for you.

- They incorporate **diagrams** to kick start your memory.

- They follow the overall **structure** of the ICAEW Workbook, but BPP Learning Media's ICAEW **Passcards** are not just a condensed book. Each card has been separately designed for clear presentation. Topics are self-contained and can be grasped visually.

- ICAEW **Passcards** are **just the right size** for pockets, briefcases and bags.

- ICAEW **Passcards focus on the exams** you will be facing.

Run through the **Passcards** as often as you can during your final revision period. The day before the exam, try to go through the **Passcards** again! You will then be well on your way to passing your exams.

Good luck!

		Page				Page
1	Reporting framework and ethics	1	12	Consolidated statements of financial performance		119
2	Format of financial statements	17	13	Associates and joint ventures		125
3	Reporting financial performance	31	14	Group accounts: disposals		131
4	Property, plant and equipment	47	15	Group statement of cash flows		137
5	Intangible assets	57	16	UK GAAP–FRS 102		143
6	Revenue and inventories	65				
7	Leases	69				
8	Financial instruments	79				
9	Other standards	91				
10	Group accounts: basic principles	99				
11	Consolidated statement of financial position	109				

1: Reporting framework and ethics

Topic List

Conceptual Framework

Regulatory framework

Convergence process

Limitations of financial statements

Fair presentation

Ethical and professional issues

In order to properly appreciate IFRSs it is important to understand the Conceptual and Regulatory Framework which has produced these standards.

Objective of financial statements

To provide financial information about the reporting entity that is useful to existing and potential investors, lenders and other creditors in making decisions relating to providing resources to the entity.

Users and their information needs

The IASB *Conceptual Framework* emphasises that financial statements are used to make economic decisions, such as:

- buying, selling or holding equity and debt instruments;
- providing or settling loans and other forms of credit;
- exercising rights to vote on, or otherwise influence, management's actions that affect the use of the entity's economic resources; and
- assessment of management's stewardship of the entity's economic resources.

Financial position, performance and changes in financial position

Financial position

- Statement of financial position

Helps users in assessing:

- the entity's ability to generate cash in the future;
- how future cash flows will be distributed;
- requirements for future finance and ability to raise that finance; and
- the ability to meet financial commitments as they fall due.

Financial performance

- Statement of profit or loss and other comprehensive income
- Statement of changes in equity

Useful in enabling users to:

- assess potential changes in the entity's economic resources in the future;
- predict the entity's capacity to generate case from its existing resource base; and
- form judgments about the effectiveness with which additional resources might be employed.

Changes in financial position

- Statement of cash flows

Information on the generation and use of cash is useful in evaluating the entity's ability to generate cash and its need to use what is generated.

Qualitative characteristics of useful financial information

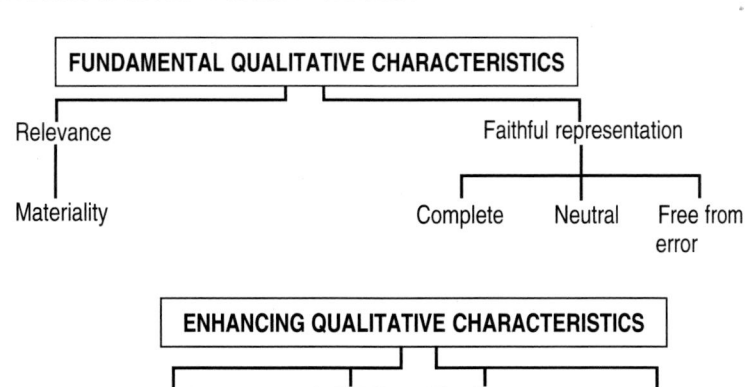

Elements of the financial statements

Asset	A present economic resource controlled by the entity as a result of past events. An economic resource is a right that has the potential to produce economic benefits.
Liability	A present obligation of the entity to transfer an economic resource as a result of past events.
Equity	The residual interest in the assets of the entity after deducting all its liabilities.
Income	Increases in assets, or decreases in liabilities, that result in increases in equity, other than those relating to contributions from holders of equity claims.
Expenses	Decreases in assets, or increases in liabilities, that results in decreases in equity other than those relating to distributions to holders of equity claims.

Recognition of elements of financial statements

Recognition is the process of capturing for inclusion in the financial statements an item that meets the definition of one of the elements.

The *Conceptual Framework* only allows items to be recognised in the financial statements if:

- The items meets the definition of an element; and

- Recognition of that element provides users of the financial statements with information that is useful, ie, it provides:

  - Relevant information about the elements

  - A faithful representation of the element

Measurement

Historical cost – based on the price of the transaction or other event that gave rise to the element

Current value measurement bases are:

- Fair value – the price that would be received to sell an asset, or paid to transfer a liability, in an orderly transaction between market participants at the measurement date

- Value in use – assesses the likely future value of the asset within an entity

- Current cost – the cost of an equivalent asset at the measurement date, comprising the consideration that would be paid at the measurementdate, plus the transaction costs that would be incurred at that date.

Regulatory framework

International Standards

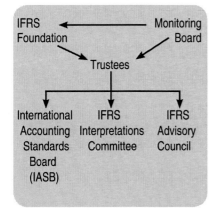

IFRS Foundation ← Monitoring Board

IFRS Foundation → Trustees ← Monitoring Board

Trustees →
- International Accounting Standards Board (IASB)
- IFRS Interpretations Committee
- IFRS Advisory Council

European Union

Since 2005 all EU listed companies have been required to apply IFRS.

UK unquoted companies are permitted (but not required) to adopt IFRS.

Objective of the IASB

A key aim is to:

develop a single set of high-quality, understandable, enforceable and globally accepted financial reporting standards

The procedure for issuing an IFRS can be summarised as follows.

1. During the early stages of a project, the IASB may establish an **Advisory Committee** to give advice on issues arising in the project. Consultation with the Advisory Committee and the IFRS Advisory Council occurs throughout the project.

2. IASB may develop and publish a **Discussion Paper** for public comment.

3. Following the receipt and review of comments, IASB develops and publishes an **Exposure Draft** for public comment.

4. Following the receipt and review of comments, the IASB issues a final **International Financial Reporting Standard**.

Convergence

The drive towards the worldwide harmonisation of financial reporting is mainly due to:

- increased globalisation of trade and of capital markets

- information technology development provides companies with the communications to take advantage of harmonisation

The benefits of convergence include:

- investors/lenders understand the financial statements better
- encouraging investment growth
- improving the quality of financial reporting
- reducing the time and cost of preparing financial statements

Progress with harmonisation

- In some countries IFRS must be applied without modification (eg, South Korea).
- In other countries IFRS are adopted to be local GAAP, sometimes with minor amendments (eg, China).
- Convergence with the US has not yet been achieved.

In the UK FRS 102 *The Financial Reporting Standard Applicable in the UK and Republic of Ireland* has replaced the majority of UK accounting standards and adopts an IFRS-based framework.

Limitations of financial statements

A number of factors may make financial statements less reliable than they appear:

- Conventionalised representation (financial statements are highly standardised and highly aggregated – this may reduce their usefulness)

- Backward-looking (yet users of the financial statements often base their decisions on expectations about the future)

- Financial statements do not include items which do not meet the definitions of the elements as defined by the IASB *Conceptual Framework* (eg, internally generated goodwill)

International

- IAS 1 requires financial statements to **present fairly** the position and performance of a company.
- This will usually be true if IFRS is adhered to.
- Departure from IFRS is only allowed in very rare cases and where compliance with IFRS would be so misleading as to conflict with the *Conceptual Framework*.
- Where departure is made, entity must provide detailed disclosure explaining the nature, reasons and impact of the departure.

UK

- CA 2006 requires that financial statements give a **true and fair view**:
  - True = factual accuracy
  - Fair = objective and unbiased
- If compliance with standards would not give true and fair view: statutory 'true and fair override'
- Where the true and fair override is evoked, the Companies Act requires disclosure of:
  - Particulars of departure
  - Reasons for the departure
  - Financial effect

Code of Ethics

This lays out ICAEW's guidance on the ethics and behaviour required by all members and **students**. The Code (which was updated in 2020) is based upon the IESBA Code of Ethics.

Integrity	To be straightforward and honest in all professional and business relationships.
Objectivity	Not to compromise professional or business judgements because of bias, conflict of interest or undue influence of others.
Professional competence and due care	To attain and maintain professional knowledge and skill at the level required to ensure that a client or employing organisation receives competent professional service.
Confidentiality	To respect the confidentiality of information acquired as a result of professional and business relationships.
Professional behaviour	To comply with relevant laws and regulations and avoid any conduct that the professional accountant knows or should know might discredit the profession.

Compliance with the fundamental principles may potentially be threatened by a broad range of circumstances:

Threats

- **Self-interest** threat, eg, financial interests, incentive compensation arrangements, undue dependence on fees

- **Self-review** threat, eg, data being reviewed by the same person responsible for preparing it

- **Advocacy** threat, eg, acting as an advocate on behalf of an assurance client in litigation or disputes with third parties

- **Familiarity** threat, eg, former partner of the firm being a director or officer of the client

- **Intimidation** threat, eg, threat of dismissal or replacement, being pressured to reduce inappropriately the extent of work performed in order to reduce fees

Two broad categories of safeguards which may elimate or reduce threats to an acceptable level:

Safeguards created by the profession, legislation or regulation	Standards in the work environment
eg,	eg,
■ Educational, training and experience requirements for entry into the profession ■ Continuing professional development requirements ■ Professional standards	■ Organisation's ethics and conduct programmes ■ Strong internal controls ■ Leadership – stresses importance of ethics and expectation that employees will act in a ethical manner

Notes

2: Format of financial statements

Topic List

IAS 1, *Presentation of Financial Statements*

IAS 12, *Income Taxes*

IAS 7, *Statement of Cash Flows*

UK GAAP comparison

This chapter covers the necessary material to help you to prepare useful financial statements. We start with a reminder of the formats for financial statements and then move onto additional areas.

IAS 1, *Presentation of Financial Statements*

- Applies to all general purposes financial statements
- Sets out minimum content for recognition, measurement and disclosures
- May be applied to not-for-profit entities

Components of financial statements

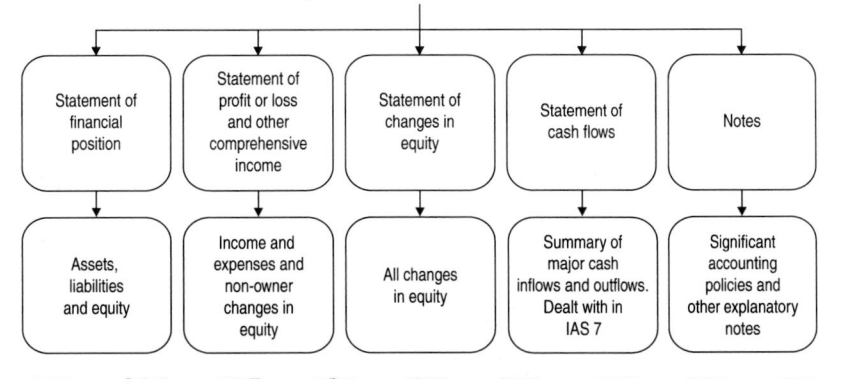

IAS 1 considerations

- Fair presentation
- Going concern – underlying assumption
- Accruals basis of accounting
- Consistency of presentation
- Materiality and aggregation
- Offsetting – not permitted unless specifically allowed or required by a standard
- Comparative information
- Disclosure of accounting policies

ABC CO
STATEMENT OF FINANCIAL POSITION
AS AT 31 DECEMBER 20X2

	20X2 £	20X1 £
Assets		
Non-current assets		
Property, plant and equipment	X	X
Intangible assets	X	X
Investments	X	X
	X	X
Current assets		
Inventories	X	X
Trade and other receivables	X	X
Investments	X	X
Cash and cash equivalents	X	X
	X	X
Total assets	X	X
	==	==

ABC CO
STATEMENT OF FINANCIAL POSITION
AS AT 31 DECEMBER 20X2 (cont)

	20X2 £	20X2 £	20X1 £	20X1 £
Equity and liabilities				
Equity attributable to owners of the parent				
Ordinary share capital	X		X	
Preference share capital	X		X	
Share premium account	X		X	
Revaluation surplus	X		X	
Retained earnings	X		X	
		$\overline{X}$		$\overline{X}$
Non-controlling interest		X		X
Total equity		$\overline{\overline{X}}$		$\overline{\overline{X}}$
Non-current liabilities				
Preference share capital	X		X	
Lease liabilities	X		X	
Borrowings	X		X	
		$\overline{X}$		$\overline{X}$
Current liabilities				
Trade and other payables	X		X	
Dividends payable	X		X	
Taxation	X		X	
Provisions	X		X	
Borrowings	X		X	
	$\overline{X}$		$\overline{X}$	
		X		X
Total equity and liabilities		$\overline{\overline{X}}$		$\overline{\overline{X}}$

ABC CO
STATEMENT OF PROFIT OR LOSS
FOR THE YEAR ENDED 31 DECEMBER 20X2

	20X2	20X1
	£	£
Revenue	X	X
Cost of sales	(X)	(X)
Gross profit	X	X
Other income	X	X
Distribution costs	(X)	(X)
Administrative expenses	(X)	(X)
Other expenses	(X)	(X)
Profit/(loss) from operations	X	X
Finance costs	(X)	(X)
Share of profit/(losses) of associates	X	X
Profit/(loss) before tax	X	X
Income tax expense	(X)	(X)
Profit/(loss) for the year from continuing operations	X	X
Profit/(loss) for the year from discontinued operations	(X)	—
Profit/(loss) for the year	X	X

IAS 1, Presentation of Financial Statements

IAS 12, Income Taxes

IAS 7, Statement of Cash Flows

UK GAAP comparison

ABC CO
STATEMENT OF PROFIT OR LOSS AND OTHER COMPREHENSIVE INCOME FOR THE YEAR ENDED 31 DECEMBER 20X2

	20X2 £	20X1 £
Profit/(loss) for the year	X	X
Other comprehensive income:		
Gains on property revaluation	X	X
Share of other comprehensive income of associates	X	X
Income tax relating to components of other comprehensive income	(X)	(X)
Total comprehensive income for the year	X	X
Profit attributable to:		
Owners of the parent	X	X
Non-controlling interest	X	X
	X	X
Total comprehensive income attributable to:		
Owners of the parent	X	X
Non-controlling interest	X	X
	X	X

2: Format of financial statements

IAS 12, *Income Taxes*

IAS 12 covers current tax. Current tax is fairly easy.

Tax charge	
Current tax	X
Under-/over-statement of prior periods	X/(X)
Share of tax of associates	X
	X

Current tax: an estimate of income tax payable for the current year.

Under-/over-statement of prior periods: as the income tax charge on taxable profits is only an estimate, there may be adjustments required in the next accounting period.

Indirect method

STATEMENT OF CASH FLOWS FOR YEAR ENDED 31.12.X1

Cash flows from operating activities

Net profit before taxation	X
Adjustments for	
Depreciation	X
Investment income	(X)
Interest expense	X
Operating profit before working capital changes	X
Increase in trade and other receivables	(X)
Decrease in inventories	X
Decrease in trade payables	(X)
Cash generated from operations	X
Interest paid	(X)
Income taxes paid	(X)
Net cash from operating activities	X

Cash generated from operations can be presented separately as a note to the statement of cash flows.

Net cash from operating activities brought forward		X
Cash flows from investing activities		
Purchase of property, plant and equipment	(X)	
Proceeds from sale of equipment	X	
Interest received	X	
Dividends received	X	
		(X)
Cash flows from financing activities		
Proceeds from issuance of share capital	X	
Proceeds from long-term borrowings	X	
Payment of lease liabilities	(X)	
Dividends paid	(X)	
Net cash used in financing activities		(X)
Net increase in cash and cash equivalents		X
Cash and cash equivalents at beginning of period		X
Cash and cash equivalents at end of period		X

Cash equivalents: short-term, highly liquid investments that are readily convertible to known amounts of cash and which are subject to an insignificant risk of changes in value.

Note. Cash and cash equivalents

Cash and cash equivalents consist of cash on hand and balances with banks, and investments in money market instruments. Cash and cash equivalents included in the cash flow statement comprise the following amounts.

	20X1	20X0
	£m	£m
Cash on hand and balances with banks	X	X
Short-term investments	X	X
Cash and cash equivalents	X	X

Direct method

The operating activities element of the statement of cash flows is different.

	£'000
Cash flows from operating activities	
Cash receipts from customers	X
Cash paid to suppliers and employees	(X)
Cash generated from operations	X
Interest paid	(X)
Income taxes paid	(X)
Net cash from operating activities	X

Standard workings

TAX PAID

		Deferred tax b/d	X
∴ Tax paid	X	Income tax b/d	X
		Charge for year	X
Deferred tax c/d	X		
Income tax c/d	X		
	X		X

LEASE LIABILITY

∴ Lease payments	X	B/d liability	
		< 1 year	X
		> 1 year	X
C/d liability		New lease in	
< 1 year	X	year	X
> 1 year	X		
	X		X

NON-CURRENT ASSETS (carrying amount)

Bal b/d	X	Depreciation	X
Revaluation	X		
∴ Addition	X		
		Bal c/d	X
	X		X

Benefits of Statements of Cash Flows

Extra information

Extra information not found in other primary statements:

- Relationships between profit and cash shown.

- Cash equivalents are included in cash balances, giving a better picture of the liquidity of the company.

- Financing inflows and outflows must be shown, rather than simply passed through reserves.

Examining relationships

- Cash flow gearing: compare operating cash flows and financing flows, particularly borrowing.

- Operating cash flows to investment flows: match cash recovery from investment to investment.

- Investment to distribution: indicates the proportion of total cash outflow designated specifically to investor return and reinvestment.

UK GAAP comparison

In the UK the presentation of financial statements is dealt with in the Companies Act 2006 and FRS 102, *The Financial Reporting Standard Applicable in the UK and Republic of Ireland*.

3: Reporting financial performance

Topic List

IAS 8, *Accounting Policies, Changes in Accounting Estimates and Errors*

IFRS 5, *Non-Current Assets Held for Sale and Discontinued Operations*

IAS 21, *The Effects of Changes in Foreign Exchange Rates*

IAS 24, *Related Party Disclosures*

IAS 33, *Earnings Per Share*

Distributable profits

UK GAAP comparison

This chapter is largely concerned with the statement of profit or loss. There is no one single IFRS Standard concerned with reporting financial performance.

IAS 8, *Accounting Policies, Changes in Accounting Estimates and Errors*

Overview

- **Selection and application** of accounting policies guidance
- Information published regarding the **accounting policies** adopted by all entities
- **Common approach** to changes in accounting policies, accounting estimates and correction of errors
- **Restrictions** on when accounting policies may be changed by the entity
- **Disclosure** requirements

Accounting policies

Accounting policies are the specific principles, bases, conventions, rules and practices applied by an entity in preparing and presenting statements.

An entity must follow the IFRS which applies to that transaction when determining its accounting policies.

In the absence of a Standard or Interpretation covering a specific transaction, other event or condition, management uses its **judgement** to develop an accounting policy which results in information that is relevant and reliable, considering in the following order:

- Standards or Interpretations dealing with similar and related issues
- The *Conceptual Framework* definitions and recognition criteria
- Other national GAAPs based on a similar *Conceptual Framework* (providing the treatment does not conflict with extant Standards, Interpretations or the *Conceptual Framework*)

Changes in accounting policy

Only allowed if:

- Required by standard or interpretation
- If the change will provide more relevant or reliable information about events or transactions

Accounting treatment:

- Apply **retrospectively**
- Restate prior year P/L and statement of FP
- Restate opening balance of retained earnings for earliest period presented
- Include as second line of statement of changes in equity for earliest period presented

Changes in accounting estimates

Apply **prospectively**, ie, in the current period (and future periods if also affected).

Prior period errors

Omissions from and misstatements in the entity's financial statements for one or more periods.

Correct material prior-period errors retrospectively in the first set of financial statements authorised for issue after their discovery:

- Restate comparative amounts for each prior period presented in which the error occurred.

- Restate the opening balances of assets, liabilities and equity for the earliest prior period presented if the error occurred before that.

- Include any adjustment to opening equity as the second line of the statement of changes in equity if the error occurred before the start of the earliest period presented.

- Disclose the nature of the error and the amount of the correction to prior periods for each line item in each period affected.

Where it is impracticable to determine the period-specific effects or the cumulative effect of the error, the entity corrects the error from the earliest period/date practicable (and discloses that fact).

IFRS 5, *Non-current Assets Held for Sale and Discontinued Operations*

Objectives

- Definition of discontinued activities
- Interaction with IAS 36 & IAS 37

Definitions

Discontinued operation	A component of an entity that either has been disposed of or is classified as held for sale and:
	(a) Represents a separate major line of business or geographical area of operations;
	(b) Is part of a single co-ordinated plan to dispose of a separate major line of business or geographical area of operations; or
	(c) Is a subsidiary acquired exclusively with a view to resale.
Component of an entity	Operations and cash flows that can be clearly distinguished, operationally and for financial reporting purposes, from the rest of the entity.
Disposal group	A group of assets to be disposed of (by sale or otherwise) together as a group in a single transaction; **and** liabilities directly associated with those assets that will be transferred in the transaction.
Asset held for sale	Its carrying amount will be recovered principally through sale rather than continuing use.

Proforma disclosure

XYZ GROUP – STATEMENT OF PROFIT OR LOSS
FOR THE YEAR ENDED 31 DECEMBER 20X3

	20X3 £'000	20X2 £'000
Continuing operations		
Revenue	X	X
Cost of sales	(X)	(X)
Gross profit	X	X
Other income	X	X
Distribution costs	(X)	(X)
Administrative expenses	(X)	(x)
Other expenses	(X)	(X)
Finance costs	(X)	(X)
Share of profit of associates	X	X
Profit before tax	X	X
Income tax expense	(X)	(X)
Profit for the year from continuing operations	X	X
Discontinued operations		
Profit for the year from discontinued operations	X	X
Profit for the year	X	X
Profit attributable to		
Owners of the parent	X	X
Non-controlling interest	X	X
	X	X

IAS 21, *The Effects of Changes in Foreign Exchange Rates*

Two currency concepts

Functional currency

Presentation currency

- Currency of the primary economic environment in which an entity operates
- The currency used for measurement in the financial statements
- Other currencies treated as a foreign currency

- Can be any currency
- Special rules apply to translation from functional currency to presentation currency
- Same rules used for translating foreign operations

During the period

- Translate each transaction at **exchange rate on date of transaction** (average rate (AR) for a period may be used as an approximation, if rates do not fluctuate significantly)

- Where the transaction is settled in the **same period** the exchange difference arising is a realised gain or loss recognised in that period.

At the reporting date

- **Non-monetary assets held at historic cost** (non-current assets, inventory): remain at historic rate (HR)

- **Non-monetary assets held at fair value** (eg, investments): exchange rate when fair value was determined (gain/loss recognised in same way as underlying fair value gain or loss)

- **Monetary assets and liabilities**: restate at closing rate (gain/loss taken to P/L)

Treatment of exchange differences

Part of profit/loss for the year:

- On **trading transactions**: under 'other operating income or expense'
- On **financing transactions**: under 'finance income/finance cost'

IAS 24, *Related Party Disclosures*

Objective is to ensure **appropriate disclosure**

Related party

Person or **entity** related to reporting entity (RE):

(a) **Person** or close member of that person's family is related to RE if that person:
- Has **control** or **joint control** over RE; or
- Has **significant influence** over RE; or
- Is member of **key management** of RE or of a parent of RE.

(b) **Entity** is related to RE if any of following:
- Entity and RE are in **same group**.
- One entity is an **associate** or **JV** of other entity (or a member of group which other entity is a member).

- Both entities are **JVs** of same third party.
- One entity is a **JV** of third party and other entity is an **associate** of the third entity.
- Entity is **a post-employment benefit plan** for employees of either RE or entity related to RE.
- Entity is **controlled/jointly controlled** by a **person** in (a).
- Person with control/joint control over RE has **significant influence** or is a member of **key management** of the entity or a parent of the entity.
- The entity (or any member of its group) provides key management personnel services to the RE.

Disclosure (always required)	■ Related party relationship between parent/subsidiaries: parent's name and name of ultimate controlling party (if FS of parent or ultimate controlling party are not publicly available: disclose next most senior parent in group that does produce publicly available FS)
	■ Key management personnel compensation in total and for short-term employee benefits, post-employment benefits, other long-term benefits, termination benefits, share-based payment
Disclosure (only required if transactions in period)	■ Nature of the relationship
	■ Amounts involved
	■ Amount of any balances outstanding at year end
	■ T&Cs attached to any outstanding balance
	■ Details of any guarantees given/received
	■ Any allowance against any outstanding balances and expense recognised in the period for bad or doubtful debts due from related parties
	■ Disclosure of the fact that transactions were on an arm's length basis

IAS 33, *Earnings per Share*

This Standard aims to improve the **comparison** of different entities in the same period and of the same entity in different periods. Only mandatory for **listed** entities.

Basic calculation

$$\frac{\text{Net profit/loss attributable to ordinary shareholders}}{\text{Weighted average no. of shares in issue during the period}}$$

The net profit or loss used is after interest, tax and deductions in respect of non-equity shares.

Changes in capital structure

It is necessary to match the earnings for the year against the capital base giving rise to those earnings.

Bonus issue

The earnings of the entity will not rise (no new funds injected); to calculate the number of shares:

- Treat bonus shares as if in issue for the full year

- Apply retrospectively, reducing the reported EPS for the previous year by the reciprocal of the bonus fraction

Issue at full market price

New capital is introduced therefore earnings would be expected to rise from date of new issue; to calculate the number of shares:

- Use time weighted average number of shares for period

- No retrospective effect

Rights issue

For purposes of calculating the number of shares, treat this as an issue at full market price followed by a bonus issue:

- Use weighted average number of shares in issue for the period modified by the retrospective effect of the bonus element

- Bonus element:

$$\frac{\text{Actual cum-rights price}}{\text{Theoretical ex-rights price}}$$

Diluted EPS

Required where a listed entity has outstanding convertible loan notes, preferred shares, debentures, options or warrants.

Must be shown on the face of the statement of profit or loss and given equal prominence with basic EPS.

- Numerators of calculations must be disclosed. Denominators must be disclosed and reconciled to each other

- Other amounts per share may be shown in the notes but profit used must be reconciled to a line item in the income statement

Convertible loan notes or preference shares

- *Earnings*

Net basis earnings	X
Add back loan note interest net of tax (or preference dividends) 'saved'	X
Diluted earnings	X

- *No of shares*

Basic weighted average	X
Add additional shares on conversion (use terms giving max dilution available after y/e)	X
Diluted number	X

Distributable profits

Private companies can distribute net accumulated realised profits.

Public companies can distribute net accumulated realised profits less net unrealised losses.

Distributable profits are calculated on the basis on the individual entity not the group as a whole.

Technical releases available from ICAEW providing guidance.

3: Reporting financial performance

- **Continuing/discontinued operations:** Under FRS 102 the results of discontinued operations are presented in a separate column in the profit and loss account.

- **Related parties:** FRS 102 does not require disclosure of transactions entered into between two or more members of a group as long as one party to the transaction is wholly owned by the other party.

- **Earnings per share:** Entities reporting under FRS 102 are required to apply IAS 33 if they fall within the scope of IAS 33.

- **Non-current assets held for sale:** FRS 102 does not have this classification. Assets awaiting sale continue to be depreciated.

4: Property, plant and equipment

Topic List

IAS 16, *Property, Plant and Equipment*

Depreciation

IAS 23, *Borrowing Costs*

IAS 36, *Impairment of Assets*

Assets held for sale

UK GAAP comparison

IAS 16 deals with most aspects of property plant and equipment.

Depending on the nature of the business, these assets can have a significant impact on the financial statements. You also need to know how to deal with impairment and with assets classified as 'held for sale'.

IAS 16, *Property, Plant and Equipment* covers all aspects of accounting for these items, which are most tangible non-current assets. IAS 16 should be followed unless another standard requires a different treatment, eg, IFRS 5

Probable that future economic benefits associated with the assets will flow to the entity.

Recognition

Cost of asset can be reliably measured.

Initial measurement

Purchase price

- Import duties
- Non-refundable purchase taxes

less

- Trade discounts/rebates

Directly attributable costs

- Site preparation
- Delivery/handling
- Testing
- Installation costs
- Professional fees

Other costs

- Estimate of dismantling/removal costs and site restoration (IAS 37)
- Finance costs (IAS 23)

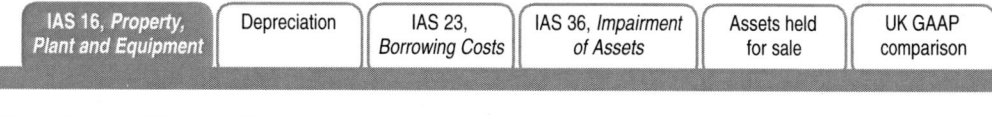

Subsequent expenditure

Same criteria as initial costs. Otherwise do not capitalise but charge to profit or loss.

Subsequent measurement

Cost model	Revaluation model	Depreciation
■ Cost less accumulated depreciation and accumulated impairment losses	■ Revalued amount (fair value at the date of revaluation) less subsequent accumulated depreciation and impairment losses ■ Revalue sufficiently regularly so carrying amount not materially different from fair value ■ All items of same class should be revalued	■ Systematic basis over useful life reflecting pattern of use of asset's economic benefits ■ Periodic review of useful life and depreciation method and any change accounted for as change in accounting estimate

4: Property, plant and equipment

Depreciation

Depreciation is a process of spreading the original cost of a non-current asset over the accounting periods in which its benefit will be felt.

- Depreciation is usually charged annually and appears as an expense in profit or loss.
- The annual charges are also accumulated in an allowance account in the statement of financial position.
- The credit balance on this account reflects the amount of the asset's original cost which has so far been written off.

The annual depreciation charge on a non-current asset is based on two factors.

- The **depreciable amount** of the asset. This is the amount which must be written off over the entire life of the asset. It consists of the original cost less any estimated residual value.
- The **estimated useful life** of the asset. This may be measured in terms of years or in terms of units of service provided by the asset.

If an asset has to be revalued, the depreciation will be based on the revalued amount divided by the remaining useful life.

Different methods:

- Straight line
- Reducing balance
- Sum of units

The double entry for depreciation is as follows.

DEBIT Depreciation expense (P/L)
CREDIT Allowance for depreciation (SFP)

This reflects:

- A periodic expense in profit or loss
- A decrease in the asset's value in the statement of financial position

Change in expected life

If after a period of an asset's life it is realised that the original useful life has been changed, then the depreciation charge needs to be adjusted.

The revised charge from that date becomes:

$$\frac{\text{Carrying amount at date of change}}{\text{Remaining useful life}}$$

Revaluation

This is permitted in order to reflect increases in asset values and is intended to provide a fairer view of the value of the business assets.

A revaluation is recorded as follows:

DEBIT Non-current asset
(revalued amount less original cost)

DEBIT Allowance for depreciation
(total depreciation to date)

CREDIT Revaluation surplus in OCI
(revalued amount less carrying amount)

IAS 23, *Borrowing Costs*

The Standard deals with borrowing costs for **self-constructed assets**. Included in borrowing costs

Borrowing costs: Interest and other costs incurred by an entity in connection with the borrowing of funds.

Qualifying asset: An asset that necessarily takes a substantial period of time to get ready for its intended sale or use.

- Interest expense calculated using the effective interest method
- Finance charges arising on lease liabilities (IFRS 16)
- **Exchange differences** as far as they are an adjustment to **interest costs**

Capitalisation is mandatory if the costs are **directly attributable** to the acquisition, construction or production of a qualifying asset.

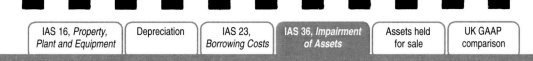

The aim of IAS 36, *Impairment of Assets* is to ensure that assets are carried in the financial statements at no more than their **recoverable amount.** Note that IAS 36 does not apply to non-current assets held for sale which are covered by IFRS 5.

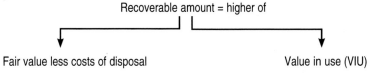

Recoverable amount = higher of

Fair value less costs of disposal

- Amount obtainable from the sale of an asset in arm's length transaction less cost of disposal.

Value in use (VIU)

- PV of estimated future cash flows expected to arise from the continuing use of an asset and its disposal at the end of its useful life.

Where it is not possible to estimate the recoverable amount of an individual asset, an entity should determine the recoverable amount of the **cash-generating unit** to which it belongs. Cash-generating units are not in the syllabus.

The standard also specifies when an entity should reverse an impairment loss and prescribes certain disclosures for impaired assets.

Indicators of impairment

A review for impairment of a non-current asset or goodwill should be carried out if events or changes in circumstances indicate that the carrying amount of the non-current asset or goodwill may not be recoverable.

External indicators

- Fall in market value

- Change in technological, legal or economic environment

- Increase in market interest rate likely to affect discount rates

- Carrying amount of entity's net assets > market capitalisation

Internal indicators

- Obsolescence or physical damage

- Adverse changes in use

- Adverse changes in asset's economic performance

Non-current assets held for sale (IFRS 5)

Criteria

- The asset (or disposal group) must be available for immediate sale in its present condition, subject only to usual and customary sales terms and
- The sale must be highly probable.

    For this to be the case:

    - The appropriate level of **management** must be **committed** to a plan to sell
    - An **active programme** to **locate a buyer** and complete the plan must have been initiated
    - The asset (or disposal group) must be **actively marketed** for sale at a price that is reasonable in relation to its current fair value
    - The sale should be expected to qualify for recognition as a completed sale **within one year** from the date of classification as held for sale (subject to limited specified exceptions)
    - Actions required to complete the plan should indicate that it is **unlikely** that **significant** changes to the plan will be made or that the plan will be withdrawn

Presentation

Assets and disposal groups (including associated liabilities) classified as held for sale are presented:

- On the face of the statement of financial position
- Separately from other assets and liabilities
- Normally as **current** assets and liabilities (not offset)

Measurement

An entity must measure a non-current asset or disposal group classified as held for sale at the **lower of**:

- Carrying amount
- Fair value less costs of disposal

Immediately before initial classifications, measure asset per applicable IFRS. Any impairment loss accounted for as normal.

Non-current assets/disposal groups classified as held for sale are **not depreciated**.

UK GAAP comparison

- There are no significant differences between IAS 16 and FRS 102
- Unlike IAS 23, FRS 102 allows entities to choose whether or not to capitalise borrowing costs

Topic List

IAS 38, *Intangible Assets*

Goodwill

UK GAAP comparison

IAS 38 prescribes the accounting treatment for intangible assets not dealt with under another IFRS. The standard deals with the criteria for recognition and measurement.

Goodwill is a controversial area. It comes up again in connection with group accounts.

IAS 38, *Intangible Assets*

Definition

An intangible asset is an identifiable non-monetary asset without physical substance held for use in the production or supply of goods or services, for rental to others, or for administrative purposes.

Recognition

Recognise if and only if:

- It is probable that the future economic benefits that are attributable to the asset will flow to the entity; **and**

- The cost of the asset can be measured reliably.

Initial measurement

Intangible assets should initially be measured at cost.

Subsequent expenditure

Subsequent expenditure must meet the original recognition criteria to be added to the cost of the intangible asset.

Amortisation

Should be charged on a systematic basis over the useful life of the asset. Should commence when asset available for use. Period and method to be reviewed at each year end.

Intangibles with indefinite useful life are not amortised, but reviewed at least annually for impairment.

Subsequent re-measurement

Cost model: cost less accumulated amortisation and impairment losses

Revaluation model: revalued amount less subsequent accumulated amortisation and impairment losses

- Revalued amount is fair value at date of revaluation by reference to an active market

- All other assets in the same class should be revalued unless there is no active market for them, in which case the cost model value should be used for those assets

- Regular revaluations so that the carrying amount does not differ materially from fair value

Impairment losses

The recoverable amount of an intangible with an indefinite useful life or that is not ready for use should be determined at least at each financial year end and any impairment loss should be accounted for in accordance with IAS 36.

Disclosures

Need to make the following disclosures:

- Distinguish between internally generated and other intangible assets
- Useful lives of assets and amortisation methods
- Gross carrying amount and accumulated amortisation at start and end of period
- Where the amortisation is included in the statement of profit or loss
- A reconciliation of opening balance to closing balance
- If research and development, how much was charged as expense

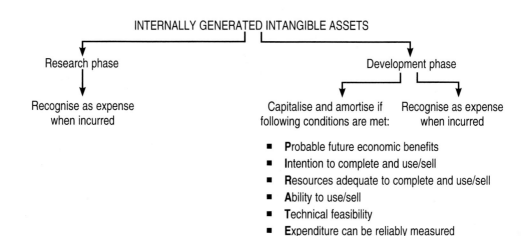

INTERNALLY GENERATED INTANGIBLE ASSETS

Research phase

Recognise as expense
when incurred

Development phase

Capitalise and amortise if
following conditions are met:

Recognise as expense
when incurred

- **P**robable future economic benefits
- **I**ntention to complete and use/sell
- **R**esources adequate to complete and use/sell
- **A**bility to use/sell
- **T**echnical feasibility
- **E**xpenditure can be reliably measured

Internally generated bands, mastheads, publishing titles, customer lists and similar items should not be recognised as intangible assets.

5: Intangible assets

Goodwill

Goodwill is recognised if it is acquired as part of a business combination.

Gain on a bargain purchase	Definition
Arises when acquirer's interest in identifiable net assets exceeds the cost of the combination. Results from **errors** or a **bargain**: ■ **Reassess cost** of combination and assets ■ Recognise **any remaining** goodwill **immediately** in **profit or loss**	Future economic benefits arising from assets that are not capable of being individually identified and separately recognised: ■ Recognise as an **asset** and measure at cost/excess of purchase cost over acquired interest ■ Do **not amortise** ■ Test at least annually for **impairment** (IAS 36)

UK GAAP comparison

- Under FRS 102 an entity can choose whether or not to capitalise development costs. IAS 38 requires all eligible development costs to be capitalised.

- FRS 102 regards all intangible assets including goodwill as having a finite useful life, with a rebuttable presumption that this will not exceed ten years. IAS 38 allows some intangible assets to be treated as having an indefinite useful life.

- FRS 102 requires goodwill to be amortised. IFRS 3 does not require amortisation but requires goodwill arising on a business combination to undergo an annual impairment review.

Notes

6: Revenue and inventories

Topic List

IFRS 15, *Revenue from Contracts with Customers*

IAS 2, *Inventories*

Revenue recognition and the valuation of inventory are important issues in ensuring that financial statements 'present fairly' the financial position and results of an entity.

IFRS 15, *Revenue from Contracts with Customers*

Under IFRS 15 revenue is recognised when **control** of goods or services passes to the customer.

The process is set out in a **five-step model**.

1. Identify the contract with a customer.
2. Identify the performance obligations in the contract.
3. Determine the transaction price.
4. Allocate the transaction price to the performance obligations.
5. Recognise revenue when (or as) the entity satisfies the performance obligations.

Satisfaction of performance obligations

A performance obligation can be satisfied:

(a) At a point in time; or
(b) Over time.

A contract may contain both of these types of performance obligation and they may be sold as a **bundle**. The transaction price must be allocated to the different performance obligations based on their **stand-alone selling price**.

Where performance obligations are satisfied over time, progress towards completion can be measured using **input** or **output** methods.

IAS 2, *Inventories*

- Inventories should be measured at the lower of cost and net realisable value – the comparison between the two should ideally be made separately for each item.
- Cost is the cost incurred in the normal course of business in bringing the product to its present location and condition, including production overheads and costs of conversion.
- Inventory can include raw materials, work in progress, finished goods, goods purchased for resale.
- FIFO and average cost are allowed.
- LIFO is not allowed.

Note. Inventory excludes construction contracts in progress (IAS 11), financial instruments (IASs 32 and 39), agricultural products (IAS 41) and mineral ores.

- **Inventories** are assets:
  - Held for sale in the ordinary course of business
  - In the process of production for such sale; or
  - In the form of materials or supplies to be consumed in the production process or in the rendering of services.

- **Net realisable value** is the estimated selling price in the ordinary course of business less the estimated costs of completion and the estimated costs necessary to make the sale.

Topic List

Lessee accounting

Sale and leaseback

This chapter looks at lessee accounting. IFRS 16 Leases provides a single lease accounting model that applies to most lease transactions. A leased asset will result in a non-current asset and liability in the statement of financial position, and expenses in the statement of profit or loss – therefore, leases have a significant effect on the financial statements.

Sale and leaseback arrangements are also covered in the syllabus.

You are not expected to account for leases from the lessors' perspective.

Lease: A contract, or part of a contract, that conveys the right to use an asset (the underlying asset) for a period of time, in exchange for consideration.

Identification

A contract between the lessor and the lessee for the lease of an asset.

- The **lessor** is the owner and supplier of the underlying asset.
- The **lessee** is the entity which has the right to use an underlying asset.

Under IFRS 16, a contract is deemed to contain a lease if it conveys the **right to control** the use of an **identified asset** for a **period of time**, in return for consideration (usually cash, although this purposely doesn't restrict the definition).

Identified asset

- The asset must be specified in the lease.
- It may be part of an asset.
- The lessor is not able to substitute the asset for an equivalent asset (and benefit economically from doing so) during the lease period.

Right to obtain substantially all of the economic benefits

Can be achieved through holding, using or sub-leasing the asset.

Right-to-direct the use of the asset (control)

Lessee can direct how and for what purpose the asset is used throughout the period of use.

The period of time is either:

- a period of time, such as years; or
- the amount of use, based upon the production of the asset, such as the number of units produced.

Recognition exemptions

IFRS 16 provides optional recognition exemptions for:

- **Short-term leases**, which are those for less than twelve months that do not contain a purchase option
- **Leases of low value assets**, being assets with a low value when new

Short-term leases	Low-value lease
12m or less: ■ No purchase option ■ Elect by asset class	■ Low value ■ Elect on a lease by lease basis ■ Independent asset

If an entity elects to apply the recognition exemptions to a lease, then the lease payments are charged to profit or loss on a straight line (or other systematic) basis over the lease term.

No right-of-use asset or lease liability are recognised in relation to that lease.

Measurement

The right-of-use asset is initially measured at cost, which includes:

- The amount of the initial measurement of the lease liability
- Any lease payments made on or before the commencement date, less any lease incentives received
- Any initial direct costs incurred by the lessee related to the asset
- Any costs or penalties to be incurred by the lessee at the end of the lease term, such as dismantling costs or removal costs.

Subsequent measurement of the right-of-use asset

Subsequently the right-of-use asset will be measured at cost less accumulated depreciation and impairment losses.

The right-of-use asset should be depreciated from the lease commencement date to the earlier of the end of its useful life or the end of the lease term **unless** the asset is expected to be transferred to the lessee at the end of the lease term.

In that case, the asset will be depreciated over its useful life.

7: Leases

Lease payments

Payments made by a lessee to a lessor relating to the right to use an underlying asset during the lease term.

Lease liability

At the commencement of the lease, the lease liability is measured at the present value of the future lease payments.

The lease liability will include the following future lease payments:

- Fixed payments less any lease incentives receivable
- Variable payments that depend on an index (such as the consumer price index) or rate (market rent)
- Amounts expected to be payable under residual value guarantees
- The exercise price of purchase options (if reasonably certain to be exercised)
- Payments for penalties for early termination

Subsequent measurement of the lease liability

In subsequent periods the lease liability is measured by:

- increasing the carrying amount to reflect interest on the lease liability (using the interest rate implicit in the lease);
- reducing the carrying amount to reflect the lease payments made.

The lease payments can be made in advance or in arrears.

Sales and leaseback transactions

- A sale and leaseback transaction involves the original owner of the asset selling it (often to a finance house or bank) and immediately leasing it back, thereby raising cash and retaining the use of the asset.

- Therefore, an entity acquires cash in exchange for a commitment to make regular lease payments without losing use of the asset.

- Under IFRS 16, there is an initial assessment as to whether or not the transfer of the asset constitutes a genuine sale.

- For this to be the case, the requirements of IFRS 15 *Revenue from Contracts with Customers* for determining when a performance obligation is satisfied must be met.

Transfer is a sale

If the transfer is a sale, the seller/lessee should:

- derecognise the asset transferred;
- recognise a right-of-use asset representing the right of use of the asset that it retains;
- recognise a gain on the rights transferred to the buyer/lessor; and
- recognise a lease liability to reflect its obligation to make lease payments.

Right-of-use asset representing the right of use retained

Carrying amount ×

$$\frac{\text{PV of future lease payments at transfer date}}{\text{Fair value of asset at transfer date}}$$

Carrying amount = PVFLP/FV of asset

Recognise only the gain relating to the rights transferred to the buyer

Stage 1: Calculate the total gain on the sale:
Fair value – carrying amount of asset
Stage 2: Calculate the gain relating to the rights retained by the seller/lessee:
Gain (Stage 1) × PVFLP/FV
Stage 3: Calculate the gain on rights transferred:
Total gain (Stage 1) – Gain relating to the rights retained from Stage 2

Transfer is not a sale:

- The asset is more like a secured loan.

Consequently,

- The seller/lessee should continue to recognise the asset and recognise a financial liability.
- The buyer/lessor should not recognise a physical asset but instead recognise a financial asset.

The financial asset/liability is measured at the transfer proceeds.

Notes

8: Financial instruments

Topic List

IAS 32, *Financial Instruments: Presentation*

IFRS 9, *Financial Instruments*

IFRS 7, *Financial Instruments: Disclosures*

UK GAAP comparison

In recent years there has been a huge growth in the number and complexity of financial instruments available. This chapter considers the accounting requirements for these financial instruments.

IAS 32, *Financial Instruments: Presentation*

Recent years have seen increasing use of complex financial instruments.

Such instruments can have a significant effect on profits, solvency and cash flow.

Three relevant accounting standards are:

- IAS 32 *Financial Instruments: Presentation*
- IFRS 9 *Financial Instruments*
- IFRS 7 *Financial Instruments: Disclosures*

Definitions

Financial instrument: any contract that gives rise to a financial asset of one entity and a financial liability or equity instrument of another.

Financial asset: cash; equity instrument of another entity; contractual right to receive cash/other financial assets; contract that can be settled in the entity's own equity instruments.

IAS 32 Presentation

- Financial instruments should be classified as:
    - Assets
    - Liability (debt)
    - Equity
- Compound instruments (exhibiting characteristics of both) must be split into their debt and equity components.
- Substance rather than legal form applies (eg, redeemable preference shares are a financial liability).
- Interest, dividends, loss or gains relating to a financial instrument claimed as a liability are reported in profit or loss for the year, while distributions to holders of equity instruments are debited directly to equity (in the SOCIE).
- Offsetting of a financial asset and liability is only allowed where there is a legally enforceable right and the entity intends to settle net or simultaneously.

Financial liability: contractual obligation to deliver cash/other financial asset; contractual obligation to exchange financial instruments under potentially unfavourable conditions.

Equity instrument: contract that evidences a residual interest in the assets of an entity after deducting all its liabilities.

IFRS 9, *Financial Instruments*

The purpose of IFRS 9 is to set out principles of how financial assets and liabilities should be **recognised** and **measured** in the financial statements.

Recognition

- Financial instruments should be **recognised** when the entity becomes a **party to the contractual provisions of the instrument**.

Measurement

- Financial instruments are initially measured at **fair value** plus transaction costs directly attributable to the acquisition or issue (or at fair value if classified as measured at fair value through profit or loss).
- Subsequent measurement should be either at **fair value** or at **amortised cost**.

Fair value is defined under IFRS 13, *Fair Value Measurement* as "the price that would be received to sell an asset or paid to transfer a liability in an orderly transaction between market participants at the measurement date" (IFRS 13: para. 9)

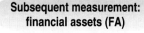

```
Subsequent measurement:
financial assets (FA)
```

```
Amortised cost          Fair value
```

- Assets held to collect contractual cash flows

- Assets held for trading or held to collect contractual cash flows and sell; can be FVTPL or FVTOCI

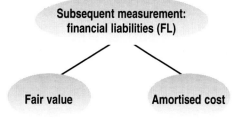

```
Subsequent measurement:
financial liabilities (FL)
```

```
Fair value          Amortised cost
```

- FL at fair value

- All others

Amortised cost

The method used in the following example applies to deep discount bonds and other similar instruments (including zero coupon bonds).

Debt issued for £400,000 (nominal) on 1.1.20X1 for proceeds of £315,526; redeemed for £400,000 (ie, par) on 31.12.20X5

Interest rate = 4%

Effective interest rate = 9.5%

Annual interest payments (4% × £400,000 × 5)		80,000
Deep discount £(400,000 – 315,526)		84,474
		164,474

At inception	DEBIT Cash	£315,526
	CREDIT Liability	£315,526

Year	P/L charge*	Actual interest payable	Rolled up interest charged to P/L	Closing liability in SOFP
20X1	29,975	16,000	13,975	329,501
20X2	31,303	16,000	15,303	344,804
20X3	32,756	16,000	16,756	361,560
20X4	34,348	16,000	18,348	379,908
20X5	36,092	16,000	20,092	400,000
	164,474	80,000	84,474	

*9.5% × opening liability in SOFP

Gains and losses
(on remeasurement to fair value)

- FVTPL: profit or loss for the year.

- Equity investments at FVTOCI: OCI for the year; never reclassified to profit or loss.

- Debt investments at FVTOCI: OCI for the year; reclassified to profit or loss on disposal.

IFRS 7, *Financial Instruments: Disclosures*

The objective of IFRS 7 is to require entities to provide disclosures in their financial statements that enable users to evaluate:

(a) The significance of financial instruments for the entity's financial position and performance

(b) The nature and extent of risks arising from financial instruments to which the entity is exposed and how the entity manages those risks

This information can influence a user's assessment of the financial position and performance of an entity and of the nature of its future cash flows.

Disclosures

SOFP

- Carrying amount and fair value of financial assets and liabilities

- Reasons for any reclassification between fair value and amortised cost

- Details of assets and exposure to risk where transfers of assets have taken place

Statement of profit or loss

- Net gains/losses
- Interest income/expense

UK GAAP comparison

- Entities reporting under FRS 102 measure financial assets or liabilities initially at transaction price. Under IFRS 9 initial measurement is at fair value.

- IFRS 9 has the category of financial assets held at fair value through other comprehensive income (FVTOCI), which does not exist under UK GAAP.

- FRS 102 divides financial instruments into 'basic' and 'other'. IFRS 9 does not make this distinction.

Notes

9: Other standards

Topic List

IAS 37, *Provisions, Contingent Liabilities and Contingent Assets*

IAS 10, *Events After the Reporting Period*

IAS 20, *Accounting for Government Grants*

UK GAAP comparison

IAS 37 should be familiar to you from your earlier studies. It is particularly topical in the light of increasing environmental awareness.

IAS 37, *Provisions, Contingent Liabilities and Contingent Assets*

IAS 37 was brought in to remedy some abuses of provisions. A provision is recognised when **all** of the following conditions are met:

- A present obligation exists as a result of a past event.
- An outflow of resources is probable.
- The amount can be estimated reliably.

- Entities should **not provide** for **costs** that need to be incurred to **operate in the future,** if those **costs could be avoided** by the entity's future actions.
- **Costs of restructuring** are to be recognised as a provision only when the entity has an **obligation** to carry out the restructuring.
- The **full amount** of any **decommissioning costs** or environmental liabilities should be **recognised from the date on which they arise**.

Provision

A liability of uncertain timing or amount. Liabilities are obligations to transfer economic benefits as a result of past transactions or events.

Contingent liability

Should be disclosed unless the possibility of any outflow of economic benefits to settle it is remote.

Contingent asset

Should be disclosed where an inflow of economic benefits is probable.

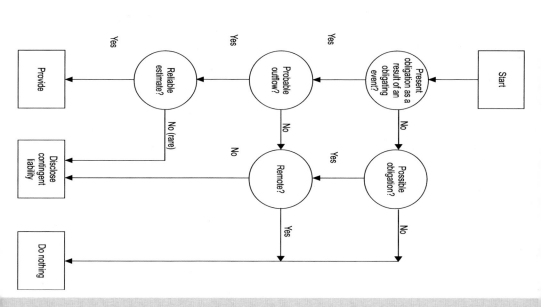

IAS 10, *Events After the Reporting Period*

Events, both favourable and unfavourable, which occur between the end of the reporting period date and the date on which the financial statements are authorised for issue.

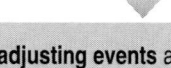

Adjusting events are events after the reporting period which provide additional evidence of conditions existing at the end of the reporting period, and therefore need to be incorporated into the financial statements.

Non-adjusting events are events which concern conditions which did **not** exist at the end of the reporting period.

Dividends declared after reporting period: do not adjust but disclose.

An entity should not prepare its financial statements on a going concern basis if the management determines after the end of the reporting period either that it intends to liquidate its business, or to cease trading, or that it has no realistic alternative but to do so.

Examples

Adjusting events	Non-adjusting events
■ Non-current assets. Determination of purchase price or proceeds of sale	■ Mergers and acquisitions
■ Property and investments. Evidence of a permanent impairment	■ Reconstructions
■ Inventories. Evidence of NRV or likely profits/losses on long-term contracts	■ Issues of shares and debentures
■ Receivables. Renegotiation by or insolvency of trade accounts receivable	■ Purchases/sales of non-current assets and investments
■ Settlement of insurance claims	■ Loss or drop in value of non-current assets or inventories occurring after the year end
■ Discoveries of error or fraud	■ Expansion or contraction of trade
■ Taxation. Rates fixed	■ Changes in rates of foreign exchange
	■ Government action or strikes
	■ Augmentation of pension benefits
	■ Dividends declared after the reporting period

IAS 20, *Accounting for Government Grants*

IAS 20 requires the following accounting treatment.

Grants related to income

Either show as credit in profit or loss (other income) **or** deduct in reporting the related expense.

Disclosures

- Accounting policy
- Nature and extent of grants recognised
- Unfulfilled conditions and other contingencies relating to grants recognised

Grants related to assets

Treat as deferred income and credit to profit or loss on systematic rational basis over useful life of asset **or** deduct grant in arriving at carrying amount of asset and recognise as income over asset's life by means of reduced depreciation charge.

Recognise only when reasonable assurance that any conditions will be met and monies received.

UK GAAP comparison

- Under FRS 102 a dividend declared on equity shares after the year end may be presented as a segregated component of retained earnings. Under IAS 10 it is merely disclosed in the notes.

- FRS 102 accounts for government grants using the performance model or the accrual model. The IAS 20 approach of deducting the grant from the carrying amount of the asset is not permitted.

10: Group accounts: basic principles

Topic List

Context for group accounts

The single entity concept

Control and ownership

IFRS 3, *Business Combinations*

Non-controlling interest

Disclosure

This chapter introduces key principles of group accounting. Group accounts treat the individual companies as a single economic entity.

Context for group accounts

A **group** is formed when one company buys shares in another company which gives it a **controlling** interest. Group accounts present the group as though it were a **single economic entity**.

Group accounts comprise:

- Consolidated statement of financial position
- Consolidated statement of profit or loss and other comprehensive income
- Consolidated statement of changes in equity
- Consolidated statement of cash flows
- Notes to the accounts and comparative figures

Context for group accounts	The single entity concept	Control and ownership	IFRS 3, *Business Combinations*	Non-controlling interest	Disclosure

Consolidation applies the single entity concept

Legal form
Each company is a separate legal person

⟷

Economic substance
The parent and subsidiaries are a single entity

This presents a true and fair view of the group to the parent company shareholders.

Individual parent company financial statements

Consolidated financial statements

Investment in subsidiary shown in statement of financial position → Replaced by addition of subsidiary's net assets in consolidated statement of financial position

Dividend income from subsidiary shown in profit or loss → Replaced by addition of subsidiary's revenue and costs in consolidated statement of profit or loss

Definitions

IFRS 10, *Consolidated Financial Statements* provides the definition of control as follows:

Subsidiary

An entity that is controlled by another entity known as the parent.

Control:

(i) Power over the investee

(ii) Exposure, or rights, to variable returns from its involvement with the investee

(iii) The ability to use its power to affect the amount of the investor's returns. (IFRS 10)

Associate

An entity in which an investor has significant influence and which is neither a subsidiary nor a joint venture of the investor.

Significant influence: the power to participate in the financial and operating policy decisions of an economic activity but not control over those policies.

A parent has **control** of a subsidiary but may not **own** 100% of it.

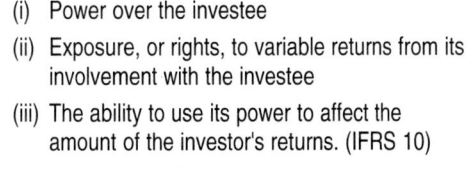

Summary of classification and treatment

Investment	Criteria	Required treatment in group accounts
Subsidiary	Control (>50% rule)	Full consolidation
Associate	Significant influence (20% + rule)	Equity accounting
Investment which is none of the above	Assets held for accretion of wealth	As for single entity accounts

Group accounts reflect both **control** and **ownership**. The consolidated statement of financial position shows the resources under group control and shows ownership split between the group and the non-controlling shareholders.

The treatment of these investments in the individual financial statements of the investor is dealt with in IAS 27, *Separate Financial Statements*.

IFRS 3, *Business Combinations*

- Business combinations to be accounted for using the acquisition method
- Disclosure requirements set out in IFRS 3

Acquisition method

- Identify the **acquirer**
- Acquisition **date**
- Measurement of **consideration**
- Identification of **assets** and **liabilities**, including **non-controlling interests**
- Recognition and measurement of **goodwill**

Deferred consideration	Contingent consideration
■ To be payable at a later date ■ Measured at fair value at acquisition date ■ If payable in cash discounted to present value	■ May be payable in the future ■ Measured at fair value ■ If amount paid is different to original estimate and resulting from: – Events occurring after acquisition – effect usually in profit or loss unless equity consideration in which case not remeasured. – Additional information becoming available about conditions at acquisition, relate back, if in measurement period. (This will be rare.)

Measurement of NCI

- IFRS 3 allows two methods:
  - **Share of net assets** (proportionate basis)
  - **At fair value:** Results in higher amount for NCI
- Choice of method available for each business combination separately

Subsequent measurement of NCI at FV

If FV at acquisition, carrying amount @ end of reporting period:

	£
FV of NCI at acquisition	X
Share of post-acq profits and reserves	X
	X

NCI and impairment of goodwill

NCI at % net assets

- All of goodwill impairment is allocated to group

NCI at FV

- Relevant proportion of impairment allocated to NCI

The disclosure requirements for group accounting are set out in IFRS 12, *Disclosure of Interests in Other Entities*.

IFRS 12 requires disclosure of:

- the significant judgements and assumptions made in determining the nature of an interest in another entity or arrangement;
- information about interests in subsidiaries, associates and joint arrangements

This information is intended to help users evaluate the nature of, and risks associated with, an entity's interests in other entities.

Notes

Topic List

Adjustments

Non-controlling interest

Goodwill arising on consolidation

Fair values

Technique of consolidation

Consolidated statement of financial position

UK GAAP comparison

The consolidated statement of financial position provides the owners of the group with more information than is available in the parent company's own statement of financial position. There are a number of standard adjustments with which you will become familiar.

Consolidation adjustments

Cancellation

When preparing a simple consolidated statement of financial position:

- Take the individual accounts of the holding company and the subsidiary and cancel out items which appear as an asset in one company and a liability in another.

- Add together all the uncancelled assets and liabilities throughout the group.

Unrealised intra-group profit

This must be deducted from the profit of the company showing the profit. If this is the subsidiary, part of the adjustment will be made against the non-controlling interest.

Part cancellation

- The subsidiary's shares may have been acquired at a price other than nominal value, raising the issue of goodwill.

- The parent may not have acquired all of the shares of the subsidiary, raising the issue of non-controlling interests.

- One entity may have issued loan stock a proportion of which is taken up by the other entity.

Mid-year acquisition

In this case, earnings for the year will have to be apportioned between the pre-acquisition and post-acquisition periods.

You must calculate the proportion of ordinary shares, preference shares and reserves attributable to non-controlling interests.

Non-controlling interest

The interest in a subsidiary undertaking included in the consolidation that is attributable to the shares held by or on behalf of persons other than the parent.

Note. If NCI is held at FV, balance will be FV at acquisition plus share of post-acquisition reserves.

Technique for dealing with non-controlling interests

Step 1. Cancel common items in the statement of financial position. Ascertain proportions of ordinary and preference shares held by NCI.

Step 2. NCI working. Add in proportions worked out in Step 1.

Step 3. Add NCI's share of reserves. Separate working for each reserve.

Step 4. Closing balances for each working are posted to NCI in the statement of financial position.

Any pre-acquisition reserves of a subsidiary company are not aggregated with the parent company's reserves in the consolidated statement of financial position.

Goodwill working	£	£
Consideration transferred		X
Non-controlling interest at acquisition*		X
Net assets at acquisition		
Share capital	X	
Share premium	X	
Retained earnings	X	(X)
Goodwill		X

* Can be at fair value or on proportionate basis.

Note that retained earnings will have to be apportioned if it is a mid-year acquisition.

Fair values

On consolidation, the **fair value** of the consideration paid for a subsidiary is compared with the **fair value** of the net assets.

IFRS 13 sets out rules which can be used to determine the fair value of the purchase consideration, the fair value of identifiable assets and liabilities acquired and the fair value of specific net assets.

Fair value

The price that would be received to sell an asset or paid to transfer a liability in an orderly transaction between market participants at the measurement date.

IFRS 3 requires that all business combinations are accounted for as acquisitions.

Fair value adjustment calculations

Goodwill is the difference between the cost of the acquisition and the acquirer's interest in the fair value of the identifiable assets and liabilities. So far we have used carrying amount for the assets and liabilities. However, IFRS 3 states that we should use fair value. Therefore adjustments may be necessary to ensure that carrying amount is equal to fair value.

Subsidiary

- Revalues assets and liabilities to fair value

OR

Parent

- Revalues assets and liabilities as a consolidation adjustment
- Subsidiary's books unchanged

Consolidation technique

Step 1. Establish group structure

Step 2. Set out net assets of subsidiary

Step 3. Produce a goodwill working

Step 4. Calculate non-controlling interest

Step 5. Calculate consolidated retained earnings

Look out for:

- Fair value adjustments
- Mid-year acquisitions
- Inter-company loans
- Unrealised profit
- Dividends
- Transfers of non-current assets

Summary: consolidated statement of financial position

Purpose	To show the net assets which P controls and the ownership of those assets
Net assets	Always 100% P plus 100% S providing P holds a majority of voting rights
Share capital	P only
Reason	Simply reporting to the parent company's shareholders in another form
Reserves	100% P plus group share of post-acquisition retained reserves of S less consolidation adjustments
Reasons	To show the extent to which the group actually owns total assets less liabilities
Non-controlling interest	NCI share of S's consolidated net assets **or** fair value plus share of post-acquisition reserves
Reason	To show the extent to which other parties own net assets that are under the control of the parent company

| Adjustments | Non-controlling interest | Goodwill arising on consolidation | Fair values | Technique of consolidation | Consolidated statement of financial position | UK GAAP comparison |

UK GAAP comparison

- Under FRS 102 non-controlling interest is always measured on the proportionate basis.

- Under FRS 102 acquisition-related costs are included in the consideration. Under IFRS 3 they are expensed.

- Goodwill is amortised under FRS 102, with useful life a maximum of ten years. Under IFRS 3 goodwill is not amortised but reviewed annually for impairment.

- Under FRS 102, a bargain purchase is referred to as 'negative goodwill', and is recognised as a separate item and presented below goodwill in the consolidated SOFP. Negative goodwill is then recognised in the P&L account in the periods in which the non-monetary assets are recovered. Under IFRS 3 it is credited immediately to profit or loss.

- FRS 102 allows a subsidiary to be excluded from consolidation due to severe long-term restrictions. IFRS 10 does not allow this.

11: Consolidated statement of financial position

Notes

12: Consolidated statements of financial performance

Topic List

Consolidated statement of profit or loss

Consolidated statement of changes in equity

Generally, the consolidated statement of profit or loss is more straightforward than the consolidated statement of financial position.

Purpose	To show the results of the group for an accounting period as if it were a single entity.
Sales revenue to profit after tax	100% P + 100% S (excluding dividend receivable from subsidiary and adjustments for intra-group transactions).
Reason	To show the results of the group which were controlled by the parent.
Intra-group sales	Strip out intra-group activity from both sales revenue and cost of sales.
Unrealised profit on intra-group sales	(a) Goods sold by P: increase cost of sales by unrealised profit
	(b) Goods sold by S: increase cost of sales by full amount of unrealised profit and decrease non-controlling interest by their share of unrealised profit
Depreciation	If the value of S's non-current assets have been subjected to a fair value uplift then any additional depreciation must be charged in the consolidated statement of profit or loss. The non-controlling interest will need to be adjusted for their share.

Transfer of non-current assets   Expenses must be increased by any profit on the transfer and reduced by any additional depreciation arising from the increased carrying amount of the asset.

The **net** unrealised profit (ie, the total profit on the sale less cumulative 'excess' depreciation charges) should be eliminated from the carrying amount of the asset and from the profit of the company that made the profit.

For instance, H transfers an asset with a carrying amount of £1,000 to S for £1,100. Depreciation is 10% p.a. The net unrealised profit is £90. This is debited to H's profit or loss and to the carrying amount of the asset.

Non-controlling interests   NCI% × profit after tax.

Mid-year acquisition   Apportion statement of profit or loss of subsidiary between pre-acquisition and post-acquisition periods.

Consolidated statement of profit or loss

Adjustments required

- Eliminate **intra group sales and purchases**
- Eliminate **unrealised profit** on intra group purchases still in inventory at the year end
- Eliminate **intra group dividends**
- Allocate profit and TCI between group and NCI

Unrealised profit and losses:

Only where S sells to P, allocate the unrealised profit between NCI and P: **Debit** group retained earnings, **Debit** NCI, **Credit** inventory

Procedure

- **Combine all P and S results** from revenue to profit after tax. Time apportion where the acquisition is mid-year
- Exclude **intra group investment** income
- **Calculate NCI** (NCI% × S's adjusted PAT)

Consolidated statement of changes in equity

As with the single company statement, this is a link between the consolidated income statement and the equity section of the consolidated statement of financial position. Here is a very simple example:

Consolidated statement of profit or loss extract 20X9	
	£'000
Profit after tax	572
Profit attributable to:	
Owners of parent	531
Non-controlling interest	41
	572

Note. Dividends paid during the year were as follows:

Parent: £97,000
Subsidiary: £26,000 to NCI

Consolidated statement of financial position extracts		
	20X8	20X9
	£'000	£'000
Share capital	600	600
Share premium	70	70
Retained earnings	324	758*
	994	1,428
Non-controlling interest	121	136**
	1,115	1,564

* (324 + 531 − 97)
** (121 + 41 − 26)

Consolidated statement of changes in equity

	Share capital £'000	Share premium £'000	Group retained earnings £'000	Total £'000	Non-controlling interest £'000	Total £'000
Balance at 1 January 20X9	600	70	324	994	121	1,115
Total comprehensive income for the year			531	531	41	572
Dividends paid	___	___	(97)	(97)	(26)	(123)
Balance at 31 December 20X9	600	70	758	1,428	136	1,564

13: Associates and joint ventures

Topic List

Equity method

Transactions with associates

Joint ventures

UK GAAP comparison

An investment can be accounted for in line with IFRS 9, fully consolidated or accounted for using the equity method, depending on the degree of control exercised. An associate or joint venture is accounted for using the equity method.

Investor's separate financial statements

- Carry at cost; or using the equity method; or in line with IFRS 9

Statement of financial position

Initial cost	X
Add/less post acquisition share of profits/losses (before dividends)	X/(X)
Less post-acquisition dividends received to avoid double counting	(X)
Carrying value	X

Consolidated financial statements

Use equity method unless:

- Investment acquired and held exclusively with a view to disposal soon
- Investor ceases to have significant influence

In these cases record at cost.

Statement of profit or loss

Group share of associate's profit after tax

Note that where the associate makes a **loss** this is recognised in the group profit or loss and deducted from the carrying amount of the associate. When that carrying amount is reduced to zero no further losses are recognised.

Associates are not part of the group so trading transactions are **not** cancelled on consolidation.

Items requiring adjustment	Items not requiring adjustment
■ Unrealised profit on transactions between group and associate should be eliminated.	■ Revenue and cost of sales not adjusted for trading between group and associate.
■ Loans and trading balances between group and associate should be shown separately.	■ Receivables and payables balances are not cancelled.
■ Dividend income from the associate is not included in the consolidated statement of profit or loss.	

Joint ventures

A **joint venture** is a joint arrangement whereby the parties that have joint control of the arrangement have rights to the net assets of the arrangment (IFRS 11).

Accounting treatment

Joint ventures are accounted for using the **equity method**.

Joint control

Is the contractually agreed sharing of control of an arrangement, which exists only when decisions about the relevant activities require the unanimous consent of the parties sharing control.

- Under FRS 102, where an investor's share of an associate's losses exceeds the initial investment, a liability is recognised. Under IAS 28 it is only recognised where an obligation exists.
- Implicit goodwill is recognised and amortised upon acquisition of an associate or joint venture under FRS 102.
- FRS 102 requires less detailed disclosures about investments in associates and joint ventures than IFRS 12.

Notes

14: Group accounts: disposals

Topic List

Disposals

IFRS 5, *Non-Current Assets Held for Sale and Discontinued Operations*

*When a group disposes of all or part of its interest in a subsidiary this needs to be reflected in the **parent's individual financial statements** and in the **group financial statements**. Your syllabus only covers full disposal of subsidiaries.*

Recording the disposal

Gain or loss on disposal is calculated as follows.

In parent company

	£
Sales proceeds	X
Less cost of investment	(X)
Profit/(loss)	X/(X)

Goodwill on acquisition which has not been written off as impaired must be included as part of profit/loss on disposal.

In group accounts

	£	£
Sales proceeds		X
Carrying amount of gooodwill at disposal:		
Goodwill at acquisition	X	
Impairment to date	(X)	
		(X)
Net assets at disposal		(X)
Add attributable to NCI (Net assets × NCI %)		X
(Profit)/loss on disposal		X

Disposal

- In profit or loss:
  - Consolidated results to date of disposal
  - Show group gain or loss separately before interest
- In SFP: no subsidiary therefore no consolidation or NCI

Note. A subsidiary disposed of will be treated as a **discontinued operation** per IFRS 5.

Dividends

The retained earnings/net assets at the date of disposal of the subsidiary are calculated deducting **only** dividends to which the holding company is entitled, ie, dividends paid up to the date of disposal.

Pro-forma calculation at the date of disposal:	
Retained earnings brought forward	X
Profit after tax to date of disposal	X
Dividends paid at date of disposal	(X)
	X

Disclosure

- The gain or loss should be disclosed separately where significant in accordance with IAS 1.

- IFRS 5 may require additional disclosure if the sale is classed as a discontinued operation.

Definitions

Discontinued operation	A component of an entity that either has been disposed of or is classified as held for sale and:
	(a) Represents a separate major line of business or geographical area of operations
	(b) Is part of a single co-ordinated plan to dispose of a separate major line of business or geographical area of operations; or
	(c) Is a subsidiary acquired exclusively with a view to resale.
Component of an entity	Operations and cash flows that can be clearly distinguished, operationally and for financial reporting purposes, from the rest of the entity.
Disposal group	A group of assets to be disposed of (by sale or otherwise) together as a group in a single transaction; **and** liabilities directly associated with those assets that will be transferred in the transaction.
Asset held for sale	Its carrying amount will be recovered principally through sale rather than continuing use.

Notes

15: Group statement of cash flows

Topic List

IAS 7, *Statement of Cash Flows*

Consolidated statements of cash flows

The work involved in preparing a group statement of cash flows is very similar to that involved in preparing an individual entity statement of cash flows. However, there are a number of additional issues to be considered.

You have already covered single company statements of cash flows. Look back to Chapter 2 if you need to refresh your memory.

IAS 7 format

Inflows and outflows of cash of an entity are classified between the major economic activities:

- Operating activities
- Investing activities
- Financing activities

IAS 7 requires these notes.

- **Property, plant and equipment**: total acquisition (not including right-of-use assets)

- **Cash and cash equivalents**: cash, short-term investments and exchange rate movements

Definitions

Cash: cash on hand and demand deposits.

Cash equivalents: short-term highly liquid investments that are readily convertible to known amounts of cash and which are subject to an insignificant risk of changes in value (generally < 3 month maturity).

What is a statement of cash flows for?

Information on cash flows assists the user in assessing entity's viability. It:

- shows entity's cash generating ability
- shows entity's cash utilisation needs

The statement required by IAS 7 is based on movement in cash and cash equivalents and can be criticised for not focusing on 'pure' cash.

Consolidated cash flows

Extra line items may be required under investing activities:

- Purchase or disposal of subsidiary
- Purchase or disposal of other business units

Non-controlling interest

Only the actual payment of cash, eg, dividends to non-controlling shareholders, should be reflected in the statement of cash flows. Include under 'cash flows from financing'.

The non-controlling interest share of profit after tax represents retained profit plus dividends paid.

	£
Non-controlling interest brought forward	X
Non-controlling interest carried forward	(X)
	(X)
Profit after tax attributable to NCI	X
Dividend paid	X

Associates and joint ventures

Only the actual cash flows from sales or
purchases between the group and the entity,
and investment in and dividends from the entity
should be included.

- Dividends received should be included as a
  separate item in 'cash flows from investing
  activities'.

- Separate disclosure of cash flows relating to
  acquisitions and investments.

- Separate disclosure of financing cash flows
  between the reporting entity and equity-
  accounted investees.

> The associate's or JV's profit after tax
> represents retained profit plus dividend
>
> | | £ | £ |
> |---|---|---|
> | Investment brought forward | | X |
> | Investment carried forward | | X |
> | | | (X) |
> | Share of profit of associate/JV | | X |
> | Dividend from an associate or JV | | X |

Acquisition or disposal of a subsidiary

Present as a simple item of cash inflow or outflow.

- Cash paid/received as consideration should be shown **net** of any cash transferred as part of the purchase/sale

- Summary note required showing:

    - Total purchase/disposal consideration
    - Portion that was cash/cash equivalents
    - Cash/cash equivalents acquired/disposed
    - Other assets/liabilities acquired/disposed

Notes

16: UK GAAP – FRS 102

Topic List

Financial statements

Group accounts

Other issues

FRS 102 is based on the IFRS for SMEs. In this section we are looking at the ways in which FRS 102 differs from IFRS.

Financial statements

- The statement of financial position format is based on CA-2006, so is presented on a net assets basis.

- An entity can present a single statement of comprehensive income or an income statement and statement of comprehensive income.

- An entity can in certain circumstances present a **statement of income and retained earnings** in place of the (separate) statement of comprehensive income and statement of changes in equity.

- The statement of cash flows follows the IFRS format.

Group accounts

- FRS 102 allows exclusion of a subsidiary from consolidation where severe long-term restrictions apply or the interest is held exclusively with a view to subsequent resale.

- FRS 102 requires non-controlling interest to be measured using the proportionate method.

- Goodwill is considered to have a finite useful life of a maximum of ten years and is amortised.

- Negative goodwill is presented on the statement of financial position as a deduction from goodwill.

- Implicit goodwill is recognised on acquisition of an associate.

Other issues

- FRS 102 recognises the qualitative characteristics of materiality, substance over form and prudence.

- Discontinued operations are presented in a separate column in the income statement.

- Entities can choose whether to capitalise borrowing costs.

- Entities can choose whether to capitalise development costs.

- Intangible assets are treated as having finite useful lives with a rebuttable presumption that this will not exceed ten years.

- FRS 102 does not allow government grants to be deducted from the carrying amount of the asset.

- FRS 102 classifies financial instruments under fewer categories than IFRS 9.

- FRS 102 has no 'held for sale' classification in respect of non-current assets.

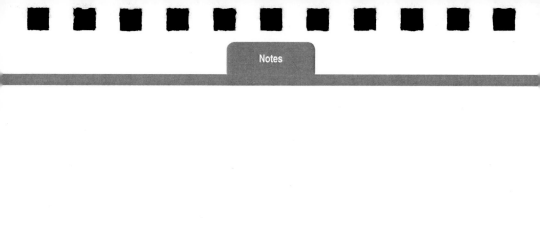

Notes

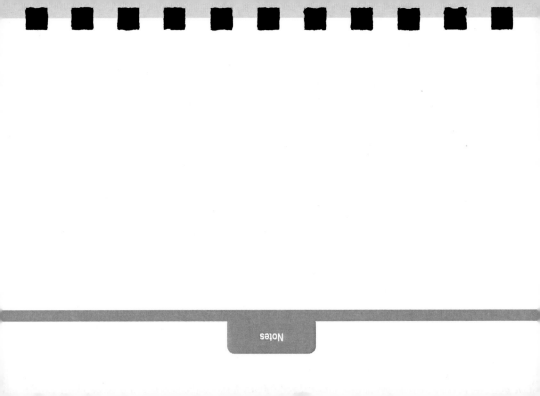

Notes

Notes

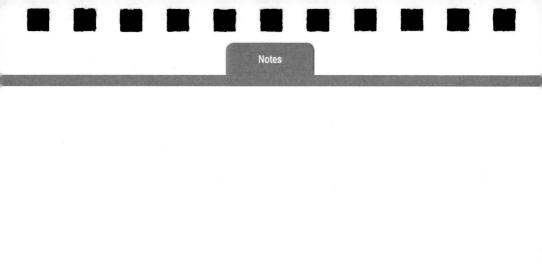

Notes

Notes

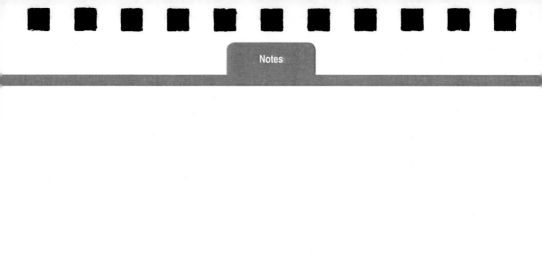

Notes

Notes